AMERICA

★ MY LAND ★ YOUR LAND ★ OUR LAND ★

WRITTEN BY W. NIKOLA-LISA

ILLUSTRATED BY 14 OUTSTANDING AMERICAN ARTISTS

LEE & LOW BOOKS, INC. ● NEW YORK

WOOD LAND

FARM LAND

WET LAND

DRY LAND

ROUGH LAND

SMOOTH LAND

LOW LAND

HIGH LAND

STRAIGHT LAND

ROUND LAND

YOUNG LAND

OLD LAND

BRIGHT LAND

DARK LAND

HOT LAND

COLD LAND

HARD LAND

SOFT LAND

RICH LAND

POOR LAND

FAST LAND

SLOW LAND

MY LAND

YOUR LAND

OUR LAND

AMERICA,

THE BEAUTIFUL!

ABOUT THE ART

HECTOR VIVEROS LEE,
"WOOD LAND/FARM LAND"

"Among my first memories of farm labor as a child is breathing the fresh, moist morning air that carried soft sounds and earthy smells. But I can also recall the mixture of sweat and dirt upon my face, and the sweltering sun at midday. The benefit of our inexpensive produce is due in part to the cheap labor provided by farmworkers, whose quality of life is filled with difficulties. Our forests and environment come into peril as there is more and more human development."

Hector Viveros Lee is the author and illustrator of *I Had a Hippopotamus*. Raised in California's Central Valley, Hector now lives in New York. His art for this book was created using gouache, India ink, and watercolor.

YVONNE BUCHANAN,
"WET LAND/DRY LAND"

"I immediately thought of a swamp: It's not water, yet not quite land. Other elements of the image came to me in a dream. I was rowing in water, green with plants. Fish shimmied by my oars, and birds chanted as I passed by. When I woke up I thought about the pollution and the battle being fought to preserve the lives of endangered species in America, as well as all over the world."

Yvonne Buchanan is the illustrator of several books for children, including *Juneteenth Jamboree*. She lives in Brooklyn, New York. She used watercolor and pen-and-ink for her artwork.

ADJOA J. BURROWES,
"ROUGH LAND/SMOOTH LAND"

"My winter scene was inspired by the great fun I had as a child skating and playing on icy cold days across from Lake Michigan in Chicago. With the temperature well below freezing, and the rough wind at our backs, we could see icy clouds come out of our mouths as we breathed. Gliding across smooth ice with new skates was truly magical."

Adjoa J. Burrowes has illustrated several books for children, including *My Steps*. She lives in Huntington, West Virginia. Her scene was created using cut paper and watercolor.

ENRIQUE O. SANCHEZ,
"LOW LAND/HIGH LAND"

"When I work on a painting like this one, which is entirely improvised, I do no preliminary drawings or plan for the final result. As the shapes and colors shift around, images appear. As I work, I am influenced by everything I have ever seen or felt."

Enrique O. Sanchez is a fine artist who has also illustrated many books for children, including *Abuela's Weave*, *Amelia's Road*, and *Confetti: Poems for Children*. Born in the Dominican Republic, he now lives in Bar Harbor, Maine. His art was created using acrylic paint on canvas.

FELICIA MARSHALL,
"STRAIGHT LAND/ROUND LAND"

"I chose to illustrate a fairground scene because I can remember how, in one short day, straight, flat farm land changed into round land with the arrival of the county fair. As a child, a trip to the fairground was one of the most exciting things to do—it was a gathering place for friends and a place to see and experience weird and wonderful things."

Felicia Marshall is the illustrator of *Down Home at Miss Dessa's*. She lives in Houston. She used acrylic paint for the art in this book.

MICHELLE REIKO KUMATA,
"YOUNG LAND/OLD LAND"

"My first idea was to show two different generations together. I was thinking about my grandfather, who was a fisherman, but I also thought this could be an image that most people could relate to, since most people's ancestors came here from other places. It's important to know who you are, where you come from, and your identity as an American. It's important to take pride in these things, and to understand and appreciate the stories of our elders."

Michelle Reiko Kumata is a native of Seattle, Washington. She created her art in this book with gouache, India ink, and acrylic paint.

CEDRIC LUCAS,
"BRIGHT LAND/DARK LAND"

"As I began this project, I searched through personal photographs and came up with images of my children playing in the bright sun with their bright, colorful toys. Then it struck me how fortunate my children are, because even in America there is the dark side of life—the poverty and destruction that impact the future of our country, our children."

Cedric Lucas has illustrated several books for children, including *Frederick Douglass: The Last Day of Slavery*. He lives with his family in Yonkers, New York. He used pastel textured with gesso for the art in this book.

KEUNHEE LEE,
"HOT LAND/COLD LAND"

"Climates can vary depending on where you live in the United States. From the heat of Hawaii to the cold winds of Alaska, weather greatly influences our lives. No matter where you live, you will always meet a young child. Our children are our hope and our future, and they carry our youth along with their own."

Keunhee Lee has illustrated *The Horse from Peru* and *Lost Times*, as well as several books in collaboration with her husband, Dom Lee. She was born in Seoul, Korea, and lives in Demarest, New Jersey. She used watercolors for her art in this book.

HUY LEE,
"HARD LAND/SOFT LAND"

"I wanted to illustrate an aspect of the America that I know well—the city. But most of all, I wanted to share my community with readers. I got the idea for my scene from sitting by an enormous window at my local bookstore and sketching the people on the streets below. The city has a lot of "hard" and "soft" qualities. The buildings, cars, cement pavements, and traffic noise are "hard." In contrast, the park is "soft," filled with tender soil, green grass, trees, and flowers."

Huy Lee is the author and illustrator of *In the Snow* and *At the Beach*. Born in Phnom Penh, Cambodia, Huy now lives in New York City. She worked with cut paper and photographs for the art in this book.

DARRYL LIGASAN,
"RICH LAND/POOR LAND"

"Poverty and affluence are realities. Yet regardless of their conditions, children will always play. I wanted to illustrate this concept by showing children of different socio-economic backgrounds enjoying the same type of play—in this case, the simple fun of throwing a paper airplane. It's in the joy and freedom of this play that these kids soar above the limits of their environments. When I look at them, I see *hope*."

Darryl Ligasan is the illustrator of *Caravan* and *Allie's Basketball Dream*. Born in the Philippines, he lives in New York City. He composed his art for this book using a computer and various digital techniques.

ANNA RICH,
"FAST LAND/SLOW LAND"

"I imagined myself rocking in an old row boat, a hot sun warming me, a soft breeze brushing my cheek. I let one hand slide through cool water, and noticed how the shape of my hand seemed to change under its surface. As I bobbed along in the calm water, not even aware of the oars gently splashing, someone suddenly flew by—on *skis!* You could put an *eye* out with those things!"

Anna Rich's many books for children include *Joshua's Masai Mask* and *Saturday at The New You*. She lives in Elmont, New York. She used oil paint on canvas for her scene.

YORIKO ITO,
"MY LAND/YOUR LAND"

"To Native Americans, the land is considered a Mother—one who nurtures and provides. In my painting, I have portrayed Mother Earth holding children of different ethnic groups. The boat on the horizon symbolizes the Pilgrims' immigration to this country. The land has always accepted all who come here, even if sometimes the different groups did not accept each other."

Yoriko Ito is the illustrator of *Lily and the Wooden Bowl* and *Jojofu*. Born in Japan, Yoriko now lives on a houseboat in Sausalito, California. She used acrylics, oil paint, and ink to create her scene.

ERWIN PRINTUP, JR.,
"OUR LAND"

"My concern is that many people overlook the natural environment in their quest for progress. Our young people are the key to the future and well-being of many different life forms and habitats we consider incidental, but which are essential in ways we may never fully realize."

Erwin Printup, Jr. is the illustrator of *Giving Thanks: A Native American Good Morning Message*. He lives in Lewiston, New York. He used acrylics on canvas for his painting.

GREGORY CHRISTIE,
"AMERICA, THE BEAUTIFUL!"

"Spirituality is the framework for this image. It's an image for anyone who can dream of golden fields, purple skies, and unity among all people in America. Children can dream like this, because the world is fresh to them. With this in mind, I tried to capture a new America, the way a child might see it—a place where people advance forward but are able to respect the land and each other's diversity."

Gregory Christie illustrated *The Palm of My Heart: Poems by African American Children*. Born in New Jersey, Greg now lives in Brooklyn, New York. He paints with acrylic.

AUTHOR'S NOTE

America is first and foremost a concept book, specifically a book of opposites. The opposites celebrate the joys and beauty of our nation, but also highlight the underlying tensions found in American society.

To open children's eyes to the world around them is to open their minds. It is my hope that **America** will open minds and inspire the conviction to face the many problems that plague our nation. It is also my hope that **America** will open hearts and inspire children to embrace the many gifts of our land and people.   —W.N.L.

Text copyright © 1997 by W. Nikola-Lisa
Illustrations copyright © 1997 by individual artists
Collection copyright © 1997 by Lee & Low Books Inc.
All rights reserved. No part of the contents of this book
may be reproduced by any means without the written
permission of the publisher.
LEE & LOW BOOKS Inc., 95 Madison Avenue, New York, NY 10016
leeandlow.com
Manufactured in China by South China Printing Co.
Book design by Christy Hale
Book production by The Kids at Our House
The text is set in Scamp

10 9 8 7 6 5 4
First Edition

Library of Congress Cataloging-in-Publication Data
Nikola-Lisa, W.
America: My land, your land, our land/by W. Nikola-Lisa;
illustrated by various artists.—1st ed.
            p.   cm.
Summary: Rhythmic text and illustrations by
fourteen different artists of color evoke the
characteristics of the American land.
ISBN 1-880000-37-7
[United States—Fiction.] I. Title.
PZ7. N5855Am 1996
[E]—dc20   96-5753
            CIP   AC